Seasons

Poems by:

Z.D. Jansa

For Ed, Mary, Stanley, and Marilyn

Seasons Pt. I: Winter in Amman

I could be pale faced and shaved
But I prefer the opposite.
I could be in Chicago, waiting on the masses to hop the
train and start my job at nine
But I prefer the desert.

I can fill this page with the stars I've seen
A million points of black ink for each a luminescent mirage
in the sky.

Has there ever been colors so vibrant before today?
The burgundy sand floods the land at Wadi Rumm like an
ocean of blood
Has there been a sky so bright at night?
Has there been tears so burnt?
In that frigid room with you,
Illuminated by the mother;
An overwhelming scent of propane and tobacco.

There were your tears
Staining the ground at Al-Za'atari
And reflected by the rage in my eyes.

My boots are tarnished
And they shall be tarnished even more.
My muscles will ache when I trek to Damascus.
And I shall hold up your robes in Victory.
This I promise you.

I have wandered through the snow at dawn.
A drunken master is a child already lived.
But it was her eyes that shone through the hazy memory
But it is the eyes of the old, the weary, and the departed
That drive into my conscious.
And that will move the rust mountains.
The wind will protest and blow me far from who I was.
The sun wraps only around the outside.

I am afraid each time I remove my boots
That my feet will not be battered enough,
That the ground will not be stained with enough blood.

And now spring has come and the bricks across my window
have eroded away
Through torrential rain and I feel nothing but inert
ecstasy.

5

My feet can synch with the beat of the music.
The rhythm flows as I progress through Mt. Hope.

Am I moving fast enough?
Can I ride my father's Chevy into the night?
With nothing in my way, but the bricks ahead.

Now I can see her face, crying in that stairwell at night.
Illuminated by the neon outside.
She is pink and purple and blue and red.
A full spectrum of sorrow, a friend.

I cannot help but feel I am abandoning the colors,
Now I see her face, crying through the black veil.
In an encouraged diaspora,
I will meet you in Damascus.

Ice Train

Sweet twinkling of stars
On a solemn winter's night
Sweet cluster of stars
Blue, silver, red shining light

I know
Plastic comes from Ursa Major
Paper falls from the delegating deities

Choices;
Paper or Plastic?

Gold and Silver are obliterated
Iron and Rust on my brow
On my crest

The plum tastes ever so delicate
From toil and blood
From dirt and mud
Streaming like rivers
To the muscle of self-actualization

Romanticized Hobos led the way
In their train-cars and junk habits
In their alcoholic endeavors
In their artisan enterprises

I was not with you in Rockland
I was not with the rallying masses
Howling to the sweet clusters of stars
Longing to be in the pack
Longing for leaders of revolution

Your loud, boisterous activities
Will not echo through eternity
Silent suffering gives way to sacrifice

The drywall seep shit
Vanity and Pride
Is born into the suburban elite

The Gods have lobotomized you
With consumerism
With frail emotions
With bitter conclusions

I was not with you in Rockland
But that is my hallowed ground
I wish to be diagnosed
To be cured
From my misplaced mind

And escape from my Ice Train

Take heed from the Winter's night
Mighty and strong is he
Yet with sounds no more than a whisper
Has you in a flee
Cowering in temporary homes
With disposable walls and incomes and people

Stand and deliver your actions
Strong and Intelligent
Without sound
Without slander and disdain
Stand on the tracks
And take my pain.

Inspiration

I could show my love, in this short poem
How the words could pour from my heart;
My mind beats the phlegm of doubt.

My face is red with fever;
Though I do not know why.

The line of snow on my countertop
Helps me take on Kilimanjaro
It is the frostbite on my skin.

The ceiling becomes the horizon;
My bed is the mountainside.

My notepad is a journey away;
I have my love to put on it.

Ainsley

Taflati, I wish you will tell the world everything.
I wish that you will shout everything from a mountaintop.
I wish that you will be strident and courageous.
I wish that you will find an ear from me.

My child, tell me the wonders that you will see.
Tell me of the ambitions that you seek to accomplish.
Tell me of the light that hits the leaves in spring.
Tell me the stars that you can travel to.

Taflati, tell me of the loves you will have, for I am no stranger.
Tell me of the love you have that is pure intoxication.
Tell me of the eyes of Bastet, which can gaze through your glossy eyes.
Tell me how you cannot possibly look at anyone else at the party.

My child, tell me of the love that makes you hysteric.
Tell me of the love that allows you to howl with laughter.
Tell me of the jokes that only you and them will begin to conceive.
Tell me of the accidental anger that they cause you.

Taflati, tell me of the true love; the only person who truly knows you.
Tell me of the love that you promised an eternal dance in Monaco.
Tell me of that first love; the one that you still dream of, years later.
Tell me of the love that haunts you, tell me of Heathcliff and Catherine.

My child, please tell me of your first heartbreak.
Tell me of the nights you spent standing in a thunderstorm.
Tell me how beholden you were to this experience.
Tell me of the Frank O'Hara realization to become more adventurous.

Taflati, tell me of the beautiful nature of confusion.
Tell me of the allure of melancholy.
Tell me of the elegance of a full moon and a cigarette.
Tell me of the graceful clichés in my poems.

My child, tell me of the life you have not had yet.

10

Tell me of the beats in your songs that synch to your breath on a winter's day.
Tell me of your father's quirkiness, I know it all too well.
Tell me of your mother's stubbornness, it may be better than you think.

Taflati, tell me of the God that you see in the grass.
Tell me the reach of your potential.
Tell me when you have lifted Atlas above himself.
Tell me the mistakes and failures and the bereavement to your goals.

My child, this is the delicacy of life.
I will not tell you of my life when you arrive.
I will not tell you the music of the universe.
I will not tell you the loves I felt.
I will not tell you of the heartache, the failure, or the faults.
I will not tell you the feeling of a caterpillar on your fingers nor the bite of the bitter wind on your face.

I will not because I love you
And I have not met you yet.
I wish that you will show me these wonders.
Show me the beauty of your first experiences
And I will show you an embrace of pride.
Welcome to the world, my child.

Haunted Well

The top was off,
In the convertible
Ford Mustang,
And I was drunk

Chill in the air,
Summer break,
Two in the morning,
Fresh air.

Just four guys,
Laughing into the cornfields
Engine noise,
Dogs barking.

Good times,
Looking for Ghosts,
Somewhere outside Morris, Illinois,
At an old Farmer's well.

Goose Lake

You can see your face rippled in the reflections
Your paddle is barely skimming the surface
Doing nothing to propel the canoe further.

Your father notices from the back
Only when your paddle slows enough to drift on the surface;
A prairie dog inverted, poking and prodding the lake.

"Son, you have to help me move forward."
"Son, you have to keep moving forward."

You know that it doesn't matter;
He is pushing you both further
Trying to teach you a lesson.

There is a curve in the road in Oswego
Bustling when the sun shines high noon
Empty as the 9th layer of Hell on a summer's night.

You stand in this road; party inside
What remains of a cigarette at your foot;
Corn blocks the lights around the bend.

Cortisol rises,
Dampened by Benzedrine and hydrocodone;
Homeostasis achieved.

You are screaming,
"Elohim!"
He is trying to teach you a lesson.

You see your face now, leathered from the sun
Rippled in the taxi's mirror,
Hagia Sophia casts a shadow that blocks out the sun.

And you can feel the power of God in the onyx paint,
In the stonework of Constantinople
Saying, "It is right to be a contradiction."

You are in your lover's arms
Head on the cushion of their lap
Her hands stroking your hair.
She is whispering pride in your ears.

Brookline Birds bellowing below.

And you are weeping.
A fetus curled on the bed.

But you will never be as weak as you were
At Goose Lake.

The House of Jansa

Stories are passed down in families
Through generations
Threefold.

You were a character in my life;
As if you were from a novel I read
Long ago.

The difference being I can see the words
You left written
Upon my own Father's face.

Funny how a short lifetime can leave
Wrinkles in the brains
Of Sons and Grandsons.

But all you are in my own life
Is the reflection of stanzas written by me.
Influenced by what I've heard.

When a funeral sparked my curiosity,
Which is why I feel inspired by
Cemeteries and Graveyards.

Florida found her newest resident among the Everglades.
Sweating and trying to remember
What a Cleveland winter felt like.

I refuse to forget you
As I have forgotten him;
If you only promise to remember me.

Seasons Pt. II: Summer in Boston

August's tendrils wrap around September's sun
Virgo energy and a pleasant kiss

How deep are the waters in Pleasure Bay?
I am as high as the cold caresses my buttocks
Specter seraphim sits on the MBTA
I walk further towards the horizon

Have you ever known what the pitter patter sound of rain
means to me?
Did you dare to listen?

Hear it now; for the Red Line beats the same
Can I time it right? If I try
Harvard tick tocks with the rhythm of my feet

Dreams for me are non-Euclidean
And mean more to me in that sense
I envy Atlas when I walk down Cambridge Street at noon.

The Virgin Mary whimpers from the corner
Sleep Paralysis
Judas was allowed an embrace

Dream, brother of Death.
Arrive with me in Acadia, mid-Autumn
They say, "The world is black and white."

And in my sleep, I see a conflagration of colors on trees
Orange is pouring through the vision as crimson leaves
scatter the doorway
I feel the warmth of the schoolhouse blankets
Covering me in the frigid cold.

Bringing hope near Maverick
When a child waves at me on the train home.

From the Window

I am watching you from the window
Trying to read your lips afar
Whisper to me your coronations

I am watching you from the window
Standing in the garden with your son
Smile for me - Consecrate Him

I am watching you from the window
Wondering what you would be like in bed
I can see that you are a Virgin

I am watching you from the window
Fantasizing about your baking
Tahini aromas in the air

I am watching you from the window
Donning white to the funeral
Sunlight gleaming from granite cloaks

I am watching you from the window
A single tear shed
While you pray for us sinners

I request your suffering
I too, suffer

I am watching me from the window
Marred by cowardice
Astounded by the Assumption

Veneration through time
Is the dust settled in the ground
Now, and at the hour of our deaths.

The Jester of Joliet

I.

I wish I wasn't so funny.

I wish you could pry my head open,
Exposing my beating organ
Flying from my chest
Up through my mouth
The words that escape;
They always have a punchline.

Creatine mornings;
Filled with ire;
Flesh and steel
Carving from stone and wood.
BCAA's, Vitamin B12, La Pietà
Calluses on my palm
Makes me feel as if I can kill God.

II.

Coming down now
In a conference room
With professionals and jokers

There is an American Flag outside my window
It is always at half-mast

I am sitting across from you
In a room
Flooded with fluorescence
With Scientists and Doctors
Endomicroscopy, Biotech, Gastroenterology

I am wondering what is in your locket
Who is it that sits so close?
What kind of experiences do you have with them?
What kind of love do they give you?

You visited me in my dreams; the words slip from my mouth.
I recognized you,
High in the colosseum

Sauntered by me slowly; sly smile;
Like you knew something about who I was.
You whispered it, passing by

I could almost hear what you muttered
Some secret

It slipped into the ether.
Damn.

I have been staring too long now;
Time to speak up.

III.

And at night, I peer at the churchyard
Where children play in the morning
The perfect view of heaven
I am listening.

I think I can hear it
Coming from my heart to my tongue

Something so quiet
Something rumbling beneath the crust of the Earth
Vibrating frequencies
-1 Hertz

If I concentrate enough
I can catch the echo of it
I can catch the shadow of a whisper

I caught it in Patti Smith's alto
Yelling in *Pissing in the River*

I heard it in *The Leaves of Grass*
In the words of *The Prophet*

Flooded out of the page and into my veins
An invisible rainbow

A slight draft wafted it in front of me
When I viewed *Fine Wind, Clear Morning*
In an old wing at the MFA

They all know it exists,
They cannot hear it.

A corn stalk leaned in the wind;
A brief glimpse.
The desert sun shown over the Prudential Center.
Or was that a dream too?

You were there.

IV.

I think I met God on the mountain
He was an old African with one eye
He spoke Swahili
For a second, he switched to Arabic
Then to a language I couldn't hear.

I heard him in my ear
When I reached the summit
The roof of the Serengeti.

He whispered,
"You're here, boy."
"You've done it, boy."
"Just rest, boy."
"You've got it, boy"
"Lay down, boy."
"You're too close, boy."
"Step over the edge, boy."

Growing to a low growl,
"You're here, boy."
"What are you going to do, boy"
"No home to go to, boy."
"Rest, boy."
"Just crack a joke, boy."
"Ain't serious, boy."
"Just crack a joke, boy."
"Have another drink, boy."
"Take the edge off, boy."
"Why so tense, boy?"
"Just crack a joke, boy."
"You can't hear it, boy."
"Rest, boy."
"Give up, boy."

V.

I fly from Tanzania around the world.
I am in a conference room.
Desert sun shown over Beacon Hill.
I am sitting across from you.
I am old. I am weary. I am tired.

Yearning to know,

Who is in your locket?

But I've been staring too long.

"Just crack a joke, boy."

For my Friend, Jacob

I do not read sheet music.
Still, the page sings to me,
Trapped in storage, the notes slice through the closet
door.
Cutting my face with teardrops over and over…

You would have loved it if I wrote a poem for you. You
would have hated this Frank O'Hara style that I chose… But
how am I to properly say all of this? You were so
opinionated… You loved me… I hope that you remember all the
great times that we had. Do you remember when we would get
drunk in our friends' basement? You used to bring
pomegranates as a snack for us all to enjoy while we, as
teenagers indulged in too much liquor, too many women on
our minds. You loved Negronis. Do you remember when we took
a turn too fast in your Ford Focus? We hydroplaned over the
median, nearly avoiding oncoming traffic. We laughed but I
knew you were scared. I was also scared of where I was
headed. I hope you realize why I had to slow down; Why I
had to move to Boston. I was trying to escape myself. I'm
not sure it worked. Do you remember when we used to watch
the girls dance in the musical? It was just you and I in
the audience. I felt like we were kings. Do you remember
when I smoked hookah in your garage? We talked about how we
each had a new lover. Mine a new woman, yours a new man… It
was so casual; I tried my best to make it mundane so you
could tell me all about him… Do you remember that? You were
so brave to admit it. I was so proud of you and honored you
would tell me first. But I left. I think that was the last
time I saw you. And when the flames surrounded you in those
final moments, did you remember all those good memories of
me? Or did you only picture, as I did when I heard the
news, the guilt of an unopened Instagram DM? After I told
you I couldn't go out for a drink with you.

I opened it, *"Sounds great, man. Do let me know."*

Surfer Rosa

She showed up wearing a white flamenco skirt
Down to her mid-calf.
Skin tanned as if she summered in Madrid
Against the stucco and brick.

I admitted to her,
"My true name is Francis,
And I like to wear black year-round.
I'm here to take you dancing under the moonlight,

In Assisi."

The Grasshopper

Setting: Bathroom of a Bar
Close enough to the mirror to kiss myself;
Have to convince myself that I love the face that I see
enough

I count the hairs on my chin, a sober test.
1…2…3…4…
Not paying attention, start again.
1…2…3…4…

I made some bullshit excuse to be by myself.
I know I'm disappointing you.
1…2…3…4…

Songs: Ohia muted through the walls,
"I've been thrashed by the hope of your eyes;
I've been thrashed by the hope of your body."

I cannot remember the color of your eyes.
All I know is that, right now, I worship them.
I worship your eyes as I worship the touch
Of the sun on my skin on breezy day.

I can picture the color, something cosmological.
Metaphysical and mythological
Neptunian and nebulae.
A color that was painted with Laila's brush.

1…2…3…4…
I may only have the power to destroy;
Days go by and my dearest friends' texts go unanswered.
I may only be running away;
Keeping secrets.

And yet I do not have the power within me
To obliterate Ego
Because I am a poet
Because I have an impulsion
To cryptically say what I need to say.

1…2…3…4…
Yet everything I write has a filter, a reason.
I cannot say what I want to say in these poems.
1st draft, 2nd draft…3…4…

If other poets and critics won't like it

I am too cowardly to say it.

If my family and friends reads these;
My solace and depression must be hidden
In fear of them asking questions.

In fear of being locked away at McLean,
Just like Plath, Lowell, and Wallace.

1...2...3...4...

If God were to know how much doubt I hold,
Would He demand that I kill my first-born son?
Like he asked of Abraham?

He made Mary watch as her son was crucified on the cross.
Venerated and vulgar.

1...2...3...4...
And so, I choose to worship your eyes,
I choose to worship the blue jays in the trees.
Because they remind me of you.

1...2...3...4...
How many drinks did I have tonight?
I do remember the days when it wasn't Lexapro
But whatever white pill someone handed me.

I am still chasing that feeling,
The Numbness mixed with pure feeling.

Is my destiny:
Drink and drug?
Pills and Powder?

Or can I live with just wine and smoke and feeling?

1...2...3...4...
Because life feels too damn hard to handle on my own.
1...2...3...4...
Between real estate
1...2...3...4...
And taxes
1...2...3...4...
And Neo-Nazis in the streets
1...2...3...4...
Crypto promises
1...2...3...4...

Social Security
1...2...3...4...
Climate change
1...2...3...4...
Women's autonomy
1...2...3...
Retirement
1...2...3...
Career opportunities
1...2...3...
Sanctification
1...2...3...
Breath
1...2...3...
Life
1...2...
Therapy
1...2...
Anti-depressants
1...2...
Global Pandemics
1...2...
Finding time
1...
Breathe
1...
Breathe
1...
Fuck
1...
Breathe
1...
1...
I can try

I can try to find my time back.
By writing these poems.

I can try like the eyes I worship.
Reflective obsidian.

Green body in the hands of a young boy.
Powerful legs trying to escape to the prairie and corn
around him.
I still remember the feeling.

I can count the hairs on the Grasshoppers legs.
1...2...3...4...

I will put him in a jar;
Poke holes in aluminum foil on top.

Staring in the glass,
"*I've been thrashed by the truth of your eyes;*
I've been thrashed by the truth of your body."

The House of Mangan

Just some Chicago city blocks away from the Wright Studio,
And the house where Hemingway was born,
There is a small gray-blue hamlet.

With a clover welcoming you, *"Céad míle fáilte"*
Greeted by dusty bookshelves and portraits
Of people from every decade of the 20th century.

Carefully curated front room
Where we spent snowy Christmas nights.
Playing the out of tune piano and drinking coffee.

Come with me up the stairs, dear guest.
Where you will find tiny bedrooms filled with tomes.
I have no idea how they snuck out so much, when being so
close.

At the end of the hall, there is a door that leads to the
roof;
I've always been too frightened to walk out there.
And a bathroom that is always clean, stocked with bar soap.

The attic is so mysterious.
I heard there were critters living up there.
I think they needed a warm home too.

The back stairs which lead to the kitchen,
Children play by running up and down.
Up and down, always.

Mary is in the kitchen, standing on the counter to reach.
What ever happened to the blackboard chef?
Reeking of Folgers, Americana.

And the basement, nautically themed.
The bathroom that only Ed uses;
Next to access to dusty, dirty storage under the stairs.

The bones of this house are strong;
Inviting all to come and have tea
Or play bridge.

Read one of the books on the shelf;
I saw Seamus Heaney, which is fitting.
Or a collection of Yiddish Proverbs.

I feel a bittersweet melancholy,
Secretly taking pictures every time, I visit,
To look back at before I board in O'Hare.

Seasons Pt. III: Spring in Karachi

We touched down at Jinnah Airport, needing sleep.

There were five of us in total:
A Greek Islander, carrying on the legacy of Aristotle and
Plato;
A young man without fear, having survived Minnesota
winters;
A healer, whose heart was somehow made of iron and
feathers;
A mentor, a man who seemingly seemed out of place and out
of time; no matter where he was;
And myself.

My hand yearned to scoop the Asian soil,
But we hurried out of luxury to a city that never ended.

The air here was filled with pollution and the Ancient
Magick,
Stemming from the night sky above the Indus Valley
Civilization.
Whispers in the wind, older than Muhammad, peace be upon
him.
Mughal Emperors had walked these streets.

And here we were to spend our days in the Sind Club,
As if we were Governors of an abolished colony.

I can see why Ozymandias was so enchanted by life here,
Why he was intoxicated by the wine and the beer.
Green Eyes shone across every face they gazed upon.

There was a time in my life that I held aspirations to
storm Damascus,
To liberate Mariupol, to lay my life down in Gaza.
Maybe I just got too afraid.

Did I pay my penance for cowardice with shit and puke?
Were the fever dreams always Metatron calling my name?
Whispers of survival confirming I'm the animal
That I believe I am.

It is my punishment to truly believe in the man that I want
to be;
Rather than the person that I currently am.

The person who writes of the majesty of desert mountains

30

When viewed from 25,000ft.
Who saw the azure of the coastline approaching Pakistan.
Retelling the stories shared amongst travel companions for
all to hear.

To see a young Mother veiled in moonlight and stars
Or bejeweled buses adorned with individuality.

Maybe my destiny is to relate the beauty of a smile,
A joke shared amongst two women who speak foreign tongues.
Or the yearning for a kiss and a hug when returning home,
Like how all good poems should end.

Of course, I then must convince you of the joy of
heartbreak.

Raspberry Beret

Such beauty, the music of ambience.
The sounds of life itself.
Shopping in a basement in Cambridge,
Dress the color of moss.

Juxtaposed with the item you're trying on,
Bright Barbie Pink top.
The clothes on the rack whisper secrets,
Swaying, scraping metal hangers, vigorous searching.

Such beauty the sounds I heard there,
Ice in the latte clanged when I set it down.
All because you asked,
"Can you zip me up?"

Can Someone Ask Me If I'm Ok?

When I buzzed my head,
You should've checked in with me.
When I grew my hair out,
You should've checked in with me.

When I said I wanted to write poetry,
You should've checked in with me.
When I hadn't posted in a while,
You should've checked in with me.

When I started taking cold showers,
You should've checked in with me.
When I stopped bathing all together,
You should've checked in with me.

When I said I wanted to be sober,
You should've checked in with me.
When I stayed out all night,
You should've checked in with me.

When I wanted to hike in the freezing cold,
You should've checked in with me.
When I wanted to move to the desert,
You should've checked in with me.

When I said I was fine alone,
You should've checked in with me.
When I told you that I found another one,
You should've checked in with me.

But who am I to blame the bee
That stings me?
When I step into the shoe,
Where he's been hibernating all winter.

Shawnee

I stood lonely in the Garden of the Gods.
Atop a rock formation;
Skies January gray.
No snow this far South.

Ol' Kentucky looms in the distance.
No hikers here this time of year;
Sound of a foghorn from a Barge
In the Ohio River.

When confronted with nothing
But the rustling of the sea of leaves
At my feet; dead on the dirty ground
And the whisper of the wind through the trees.

We do not own the houses that we live in;
Nor the businesses that we work for;
Nor the treaties our countries sign;
Nor the titles and lands that we are given.

I don't even own my name.
It is given to us by strangers when we are born,
And etched into stone by strangers
At the end.

All that I am are the senses that are happening right now.
All that I am is flesh and blood;
All that I am is a body,
Here and now in Southern Illinois.

I am the smell of must from Cypress Swamp,
The smell of sweat and wine above the pan.

I am the taste of Stoker's tobacco, packed into my lip,
The taste of the salt on your skin.

I am the sight of the sun rising from the inside of my
Chevy,
The sight of your smile as I crack a joke.

I am the sound of a bottle of Budweiser, gently placed on
the bar top,
The sound of your laughter which echoes forever in my head.

I am the feeling of the kick-back of the AK-74 in my hands,
The touch of my arm around your waist.

There is something brewing deep down in my gut,
In the sinew and fibers of who I am;
And I whisper MY true name,
Into the trees in Shawnee Forest.

In hopes that the wind will pick it up,
And carry it Eastward to the Atlantic coast,
And you will hear it crescendo in the breeze,
My trumpets and violins.

Just Don't

Don't look in my direction.
Everytime, I feel a tidal wave washing me away;
It'll be impossible for me to break eye contact.

Don't smile at me.
I don't think I can stand such intense heat;
I might be grinning too much back.

Don't say my full name again.
It sounds like music floating distantly in the air;
I laid my past, present, and future at your feet.

Don't touch me.
It'll just make me want to experience more;
To feel you to my fullest extent.

Don't kiss me again.
Was it Judas who sealed the deal?
On the lips or the cheek?

Don't get me drunk.
The truth is somewhere between this glass;
And the bottom of the bottle.

Rabbit

The bloated corpse remained
Sitting at the edge of the property.

It was my fault, empathetic.

I did not run it over,
I did not step on it,
It was not an accident.

I wish I could say I was just following orders,
But I wanted to finish it off.

I took the gun and shot it directly in the jugular.
Clean but not quick.

Its ears were coated in blood,
When the aura fell from its eyes.
Told myself I was putting it out of its misery.

But it felt the same, warmth and want,
As the time with the rat
And the baseball bat.

You Deserve Poems Written About You

Don't worry about some Shakespearian cliches in this poem
I do not have to compare you to anything
Nor are you like a summer's day.

You are late-summer cherries,
And risotto and charcuterie.

You are tequila and cigarettes,
And the drip in the back of my throat.

I only wish I had the skill to write you a sonnet,
Or many, as you deserve.

Can you lay me down in a bed of dead flowers?

Can you imagine me writing,
Clad only in my underwear,
Like Leonard Cohen writing *Hallelujah*?

And yet here I am, half-naked,
Because the words are bleeding out of me,
And I don't want to stain my shirt.

I can tell you it's not mania or melancholy,
Loneliness or lunacy.
Although my previous stanza would suggest otherwise.

It's more boldness and bravery.

The most courageous I've ever been,
Was when I told you I want you.

The strobes flashing a small smirk on your face,
My favorite thing about you.
Like you are a painting of a woman long ago,

Who has a secret lost to the ages.

Have you seen the Templo Mayor?
Have you seen Göbekli Tepe?
Have you seen the henges in Ireland?
Or the pillars of Karnak?

Me neither, so let me take you there.

To the ancestors of want and pleasure,

So, you can taste the ancient stones;
And feel the sense of wonder and excitement,
That I will feel when I see you again.

I am brave enough to write poems about you,
And to tell you how much I want and admire you,

But too spineless to title it with your name.

Ode to Florence Welch

I.

We gathered,
Adorned with flower crowns.
We gathered,
Just across the bay from Salem.

A coven of heretics
And mages and witches
Who's a heretic now?
In the Garden

Something's coming, so out of breath
I just kept spinning and I danced myself to death

I danced as if I was a whirling dervish,
Offering myself up to God,
In ritual
We raise it up, this offering

And here I was,
Bloodied feet,
I couldn't stop,

And my feet are spinning around
Never knew I was a dancer

Suddenly, I was not in Boston,
I had been transported into the past
By the magic of song

II.

Woke up in Chicago and the sky turned black
And you're so high, you're so high, you have to be an angel
And I'm so high, I'm so high, I can see an angel

Fluorescence shown harshly into my eyes
As I awoke from my stupor

Did I drink too much? Am I losing touch?
Did I build a ship to wreck?

It's as if I awoke in a memory
Hearing your songs reminded me of those times

40

When I would spend hours in the mirror, yelling,
What kind of man loves like this?

Or the times I would be on an airplane,
Heading back from a distant land, asking,
Is it too late to come on home?
Are all those bridges now old stone?

I remember it all, and yet
It feels as if I have fallen into a vision
Of where I could've ended up

I'm in the grip of a hurricane.

Or at least it feels like one,
I look outside to the skyline,
The Sears Tower
All around you the buildings sway

Sky, sky full of life
And yet there is nothing to look at
But my own reflection, screaming at myself,
You're a real man, and you do what you can
You only take as much as you can grab with two hands

So disappointing.

Transport with me to the pinnacle of civilization,
Where we can say for sure,
Every city was a gift
And every skyline was like a kiss upon the lips.

III.

I am baptized in the Bosphorus
That's what the water gave me
I am here in Byzantium

Where Theodora lives as my mistress
Crowned in gold, light of the world

I cannot see anyone but her
The way you use your body, baby, come on and work it for me

She tells me she cannot love me, the way I do to her,
Make up your mind
Let me live or let me love you

She is bound by her sacred duties
You came over me like some holy rite

She tells me that I have nightmares
I just tell her that,
There's a ghost in my mouth
And it talks in my sleep

I do not want revenge on the Emperor
I only plead with my love,
Shower your affection, let it rain on me

But with the baptism I have become something more
Something ancient
Holy water cannot help you now
See, I've come to burn your kingdom down

IV.

English sun, she has come
To kiss my face and tell me I'm the chosen one

Here I am sitting on a throne,
Under the roof
Of a Celtic Barrow

Druids blessing me
I'm not looking for absolution
Because I've found myself an old solution

To the tombs of my ancestor, I ascend,
Under the great Northern lights,
There is nothing to describe
Except the moon still bright against the worrying sky

But in the wind, I hear your songs,
In the Thames I begin to survive
Your songs remind me of swimming
Which I forgot when I started to sink

Empower me, I beg you
To the point where I can look in that mirror in Chicago
And finally say,
I am king.

Born Under the Illini Sun

I took for granted the nights
Of being too scared to dance
At Red Lion

Or Karaoke at the bar
That I worked until
Four in the morning

Or the days where the chill
Made the Morrow Plots
Stand tall and stiff

Or the debates in Davenport
The bathrooms were always a nice getaway
From intellectualism

Or the bottle of Rumple Minze
In a party in a house in Urbana
Leading us to a rooftop at night

Or the Alma Mater statue
Bronzed after the restoration
Fun to climb on

Or the bells that rang
On the South Quad Tower
Across from the art museum

Took it for granted
Because now, I am back
To loving to dance

Seasons Pt. IV: Autumn in Acadia

Let's go get some lobster in Bar Harbor
In a little restaurant overlooking the Atlantic

We can drive through Castine and Brooklin
See the trolls in the Botanical Gardens

Many years ago, I saw the majesty of Acadia,
Lit up with the colors of early November

Yesterday I saw Lady Lamb at the Armory
In Somerville

Young lovers, schoolhouse living
Across from the old church

What did you do for me?
But strip me of all cynicism
That was built up over the years
Like the barnacles on the hull of a vessel.

How could I not find some hope,
On the tips of my fingertips,
Bioluminescent algae,
Or the warm feel of your skin?

Do you remember how fucking cold it was,
In that bathroom?

Echoes of the tears,
Outside my bedroom window,
October rain has come.

I think the metaphor is usually stripping oneself
Like the skin of a cottonmouth

But there is a more apt comparison,
To the New England Maple,
That is, after all,
Where I ended up growing my roots.

Year after year I have grown
Another layer upon my trunk,
And these poems are the sap farmer
Come to tap into the truth of who I am.

If you burrow deep enough,

You will find the Boy,
Who would drive across America,
To see you.

You will find the Boy,
Who is driving to a rural gas station,
Pouting, when faced with rejection,
From a beautiful girl.

You will find the Boy,
Sipping coconut rum from a water bottle,
Going to high school football games,
After smoking a bowl fashioned from an iced tea can.

You will find the core,
Of a small boy,
Clutching a stuffed frog, terrified,
Tornado sirens ahead, cowering in the corner.

And yet all you see is the grand Maple,
Healthy trunk,
Head ablaze with crimson leaves,
Standing tall and firm.

You do not see the sunlight,
Engulfing it for five years,
Indian Summer,
Or the fear for the winter to come

Or the rings of the tree,
That these poems will never tap,
Because some of those,
Are too precious to write about.

Driving the Highways Through Charleston

A few hours on the country roads;
Many hours away from the fields of Indiana,
The bustle of Chicago,
And the gaze of the Mothman,
In Point Pleasant.

I turned onto the turnpike,
V-6 roared into Appalachia,
Halloween hills,
Costumed in dying leaves,
Transformed into the gold dome of the capitol.

Pulled over at a rest stop,
To appreciate the fresh air,
Parked my car in between,
Two MAGA trucks,
Flags waving at me in the wind.

I truly believe that God,
Shaped these mountains,
From Her breasts,
And heaved desperation,
Addiction and confusion.

I would've stayed if I could,
But *Wagon Wheel* came on shuffle,
And reminded me that I needed to
See my baby, in Raleigh,
Tonight.

I walk the line of feeling,
And un-feeling,
Obsessing over a kiss,
Needing to feel actual pain,
Bruised and blue.

Or being completely numb,
From something as small as a pill,
Junkie in Charleston,
I heard a song about that once,
Laid down and couldn't feel my legs.

I've been chasing that,
Or running from it,
All my life,
Finding just the cold air in West Virginia.

The Hunter

I have seen countless people come and go
They want my attention and talk to me
As if I wanted theirs

My focus is on the world outside
There is a chipmunk just outside the window
He's begging for it

I have explored so much of this room
Finding things under tables
Eating bugs from up high

And yet I feel trapped here,
Just watching the birds
Beckoning from the tree

Years and years of chasing a string
And fending off advances
From the suitors that come for the night

I have made leaps and bounds
At night when no one is watching
I'm sure they hear it though

Practice, practice, practice
Makes perfect
So, they say

My orange hair has turned white
Finding it when I am grooming
Sitting at the windowsill

One day, it is different
Finding the door open
In the middle of winter

I step outside to the snow at my feet
Footsteps crunch and echo through the air
I must stay silent

There is a cardinal, bright red
Against the ivory backdrop
Clear as day

I hunch over, tiptoeing to the tree
Finding my footing to pounce on it

47

And spring into the air

I fly and I fly
And the cardinal
Flies and flies away

I hit a branch
Blood coming from my face
Crimson on a porcelain backdrop

I lay there awaiting help
I don't know what I was thinking
I am a house cat after all

Fog in Amherst

Follow the Johnny Appleseed Trail
To the place that the valley opens
To a red brick tower
And the Pixies sing in the leaves

Rev the engine
Air mixing with the ignition
Through the silent orchids
To the foggy streets of UMass

Smell the gasoline
In the buildings
And the town
And the hills around

Minute Men stand vigil
Around the poets
And the scholars
And the partygoers

I was there only once
Enchanted with the vale
Veiled in clouds
Upon the ground

Mushroom pickings
Women abound
I can imagine
A Triumph roaring in the night.

Strange and Wild World

There be a man sitting in Jamaica.
Gray dreadlocks and beard,
Playing guitar on a plastic chair.
Smoking a cigarette,
Drinking a beer.

I had my first beer there,
In Ocho Rios,
Red Stripe with my brother.
The old Rasta nodded his head to me,
Strumming away the dusty interior.

Did I get too high? Did I drink too much wine?
Because that man is sitting across from me,
In Brighton,
In my reading chair,
And he is laughing.

Hallucinogenic dream,
Psilocybin nightmare,
I cannot believe it, almost as surreal,
As the hookah smoking Pirates,
That I saw in Petra.

Seasons Pt. V: A Change in Perspective

I learned something new today in class.

I learned about Hegel's Master-Slave dialectic,
Where you only truly know yourself,
When confronted with another.

But what happens when that other,
Is a pair of green eyes,
Looking at you through a photograph?

When the other seems so foreign,
But it is yourself,
In another time and place,
Another season.

How can I convince myself,
That it's me in the picture?
When everything seems so different.

And I know that even stone epitaphs,
In graveyards and cemeteries,
Erode with just water,
And time.

And my purpose can change,
And I will turn to peace,
And beauty will subside,
And heartache will wane,
And the lost will be found.

It all seems so far away,
A flower blooms only a few times,
But a song can last forever.

What I have seen,
What I have heard,
What I have felt,
It is all me.

It has always been just a slight
Change in the weather.

Acknowledgements

There are a multitude of people I can thank for the creation of this poetry collection. If I miss out on you, there might be another collection to find your name.

First and foremost, I would like to thank my mom and dad, David and Barbara Jansa. You really made it a priority for me to follow my dreams. I know I chose to pursue poetry and archaeology in the end, both of which do not pay that well, but the patience and confidence in me is much appreciated.

Second, I would like to thank my brothers, Jacob and Joshua Jansa. They kept me unserious enough to not be bothered by criticism.

With that, my sister-in-law, Bre, and my niece and nephew, Ainsley and Ezra. I don't know where I would be without their presence in my life.

To Liz Biddle and Nathan Smith, thank you for letting me crash at your place. Many of the later poems were written while I watched Puffin and Dottie.

To Daniel Balun, Phylicia Rada, Collin McQuarters, and Jacob Menard, thank you for growing up with me and supporting me through thick and thin.

To Michael Pufunt and Caleb Weiss, you guys were there the whole time. I really cannot say that anyone else is more of a rock in my life than you two. I miss you guys so much.

Special shoutout to Caleb, he took and edited that lovely picture of me on the back cover. He is a fantastic friend and photographer.

Finally, to Rachel Smith, thank you for saying you were a fan of Z.D. Jansa. It was the final push I needed to get this collection finished. I hope you are a fan of Z.D. Jansa for many more collections to come.

About the Author

Z.D. Jansa was raised in Joliet, IL. He attended The University of Illinois at Urbana-Champaign for his undergraduate degree in Anthropology. He enjoys many things in life, but first and foremost is his love for traveling, reading, and writing. Z.D. Jansa currently resides in Boston, MA.

This is his first poetry collection.

Photo credit: Author's Picture - Caleb Weiss

Cover photo taken by the Author in Waltham, MA.

Made in the USA
Middletown, DE
21 April 2025

74225416R00033